Church Hurt

PASTOR DR. CLAUDINE BENJAMIN

CHURCH HURT. Copyright @ 2025. Pastor Dr. Claudine Benjamin. All rights reserved.

For more information or to book an event, contact:
inspiredtowinsouls@gmail.com

No part of this publication may be reproduced, stored in a retrieval system or transmitted in any form or by any means, electronic, mechanical, photocopying, recording or otherwise without the prior written permission of the author.

Published by:

Editor: Cleveland O. McLeish (Author C. Orville McLeish)

ISBN: 978-1-965635-79-7 (paperback)

Scripture quotations marked "KJV" are taken from the Holy Bible, King James Version (Public Domain).

About the Author

Pastor Claudine Benjamin is a pastor, teacher, and writer whose ministry flows from a deep passion for healing, restoration, and the great commission. With years of experience serving God's people, she has witnessed both the beauty and the brokenness of church life. Out of these experiences, she writes with honesty and compassion about the realities of ministry—the victories that inspire, and the wounds that often remain unseen.

As a pastor, she understands the unique challenges that leaders, their families, and their congregations face. Her heart beats for those who have been hurt within the church and for those who silently carry burdens behind the pulpit. Her mission is to remind the body of Christ that hurt is real, but so is God's healing, and that shepherds and sheep alike can walk together in grace.

Pastor Claudine has authored multiple books and devotionals focused on faith, resilience, evangelism, and discipleship. She continues to preach the gospel with urgency, write with transparency, and mentor others with love.

When she is not writing or preaching, she enjoys spending time with her family, nurturing her creative gifts, and encouraging others to live boldly in their God-given purpose.

You can connect with Pastor Claudine through her ministry platforms and publications, where her words continue to inspire, challenge, and bring hope to readers around the world.

Dedication

This book is dedicated to every pastor who has preached with a broken heart, to every spouse who has carried invisible battles in silence, and to every child who has cried silent tears because of whispers they never deserved.

It is also dedicated to the faithful members who have endured hurt and yet remained in the fold, choosing grace instead of bitterness.

May these pages remind you that your pain is not forgotten, your labor is not in vain, and the God who called you is also the God who heals you.

Acknowledgment

I want to thank my Lord and Savior, Jesus Christ, the Good Shepherd, who binds up the wounds of His sheep and His shepherds alike. Without His grace, these words would be empty.

To pastors and leaders everywhere, you have given so much more than people will ever know. This book is for you, to remind you that you are seen and loved by God.

To the families of pastors—spouses and children who sacrifice behind the scenes—you are the unsung heroes of ministry. Your silent strength has inspired these pages.

To church members past and present who have been brave enough to share your stories of hurt and healing, you are the reason these words breathe life.

And to my family, who have walked with me through the realities of both pain and purpose, thank you for standing beside me with faith, love, and endurance.

Table of Contents

About the Author iii
Dedication v
Acknowledgment vii
Introduction: When the Church Hurts 11
Chapter 1: The Perfect Sunday 15
Chapter 2: The Whispering Voices 19
Chapter 3: Behind the Parsonage Door 23
Chapter 4: A Daughter's Silent Tears 27
Chapter 5: The Burden of Expectations 31
Chapter 6: The Confrontation 35
Chapter 7: Miriam's Breaking Point 39
Chapter 8: When Shepherds Bleed 43
Chapter 9: God's Perspective 47
Chapter 10: The Path to Healing 51
Conclusion: When Hurt Finds Healing 55

Introduction

When the Church Hurts

The church is meant to be a place of refuge. It is supposed to be the sanctuary where the broken find healing, where the weary find rest, and where the wounded discover love and grace. The body of Christ is designed to be a family where everyone belongs, where we "rejoice with those who rejoice, and weep with those who weep" (see Romans 12:15). Yet, for many, the church has also been the place where some of their deepest wounds were inflicted.

We often talk about church hurt as if it only belongs to the pews. We listen to stories of members who were overlooked, mistreated, judged, or abandoned. We sympathize with those who walked away from congregations because of offense, betrayal, or neglect. And truly, their pain is real, their voices matter, and their healing is necessary.

But rarely do we talk about the other side of church hurt—the side carried silently by pastors and their families. While members may magnify their own pain, pastors are often expected to minimize theirs. Members can leave the church when they are hurt; pastors cannot. Members can voice their grievances; pastors must often endure in silence. Members can choose to stop serving; pastors are bound by calling, duty, and covenant.

What many fail to see is that behind every pulpit stands a human being—a shepherd who bleeds. Behind every sermon preached is a man or woman who may have cried all night before standing to declare, "Thus saith the Lord." Behind every smile is a family who sacrifices quietly, who often feels invisible, and who endures scrutiny that few others could bear.

This book tells their story.

It tells the story of a pastor who gave his all, only to be told it wasn't enough. Of a wife who bore the sting of whispers and the weight of loneliness. Of children who grew up in the shadows of gossip and judgment, their innocent hearts scarred by words meant for their father. It tells the story of a congregation wrestling with its own needs and disappointments, often blind to the cost of the one who serves them.

But this is not only a story of brokenness. It is also a story of grace.

Yes, church hurt is real, but so is church healing. This book is an invitation to see both sides: the pain of the pew and the pain of the pulpit. It is a call to compassion, to forgiveness, and to reconciliation. It is a reminder that the church is not built on perfect people, but on a perfect Savior who binds up the wounds of His people—shepherds and sheep alike.

My prayer is that as you journey through these pages, you will see yourself in the story. Perhaps you will recognize your own hurt in the whispers of the congregation. Perhaps you will see the quiet tears of your pastor in a new light. Perhaps you will finally understand the weight carried by a spouse, or the silent tears of a pastor's child.

And above all, I pray you will see the heart of God—the Shepherd who never forgets, who never overlooks, and who never minimizes your pain.

To every pastor who has felt invisible, to every spouse who has carried burdens in silence, to every child who has cried unseen tears, and to every member who has wrestled with disappointment in the church, this book is for you. May it be a mirror, a balm, and a bridge to healing.

Because while the church may wound, Christ still heals. And His love is greater than every hurt.

Chapter 1

The Perfect Sunday

The sun streamed gently through the stained-glass windows of Grace Tabernacle Church. Inside, the choir lifted their voices in harmony, ushering in a presence that was almost tangible. The sanctuary was alive with expectancy. Mothers clapped their hands, children swayed, and deacons tapped their feet to the rhythm of worship.

Pastor David stood at the pulpit, Bible open, his voice resonating with conviction.

"Church, weeping may endure for a night, but joy—oh, joy—comes in the morning!"

A ripple of amens and hallelujahs echoed back. For a moment, it felt like heaven had bent low to embrace the congregation.

Rachel, his teenage daughter, sat near the front with her mother, Miriam. She watched her father preach with pride in her eyes. To her, he was more than a pastor—he was Dad. The man who tucked her in at night, prayed over her exams, and still found ways to smile, even when he came home tired.

By the time the altar call came, the sanctuary was filled with tears and uplifted hands. A young man gave his life to Christ that morning. Pastor David's heart swelled with gratitude. He whispered a silent prayer: *"Thank You, Lord. This is why I do what I do."*

The benediction was spoken, and the crowd slowly filtered out. Smiles, hugs, and the aroma of home-cooked Sunday dinners filled the air. To the untrained eye, it had been a perfect Sunday. But beneath the surface, whispers had already begun.

Near the back of the sanctuary, Sister Clara leaned toward another member. "He preached good, but did you notice he didn't visit Sister Helen this week after her surgery? A pastor should make time for his flock. We all have needs."

Another sister nodded, sighing dramatically. "And did you hear he canceled the midweek Bible class last month because of 'family time'? Family is important, but the church is his first responsibility."

Their words, quiet as they were, spread like a draft through the hallway. What began as murmurs turned into conversations, and soon into quiet criticisms carried home around dining tables.

Meanwhile, Pastor David shook hands at the door, smiling, blessing each member as they left. He didn't hear the whispers, but Miriam sensed them. She saw the guarded looks, the subtle coldness from certain members. After years of ministry, she had learned to read between the lines.

As they walked toward the car, Rachel tugged at her mother's sleeve. "Mom, did Dad do something wrong? I heard Sister Clara saying he doesn't care about people."

Miriam forced a smile, brushing her daughter's hair back. "No, sweetheart. Your father cares more than they'll ever know."

Pastor David didn't speak. He simply looked up at the sky, his heart heavy. He had given his all that morning—heart, soul, and strength. Yet somehow, it still wouldn't be enough.

The perfect Sunday had ended, but the storm of criticism was only beginning.

REFLECTION

The pulpit shows only one side of the story. While members magnify their disappointments, the shepherd often bleeds quietly. Every sermon preached costs more than words—it costs unseen tears, sacrifice, and strength.

Chapter 2

The Whispering Voices

The fellowship hall buzzed with laughter as members lingered over coffee and pastries after service. On the surface, everything seemed warm and pleasant, but in one corner of the room, the whispers had begun to spread.

Sister Clara leaned in close to a younger woman, her voice lowered but sharp. "You know, pastor preached well this morning, but I can't help noticing his visits are… lacking. Sister Helen's surgery came and went, and where was he?"

The younger woman nodded slowly, hesitant but swayed by Clara's confidence.

Clara continued, "And the Bible study—he canceled for family time. I'm not saying family isn't important, but when you're the shepherd, the sheep come first. If we start letting family be an excuse, where does it end?"

Nearby, Ethan, a long-time member, caught fragments of the conversation. He'd been feeling overlooked himself—his request for prayer at work had gone unanswered during midweek service.

The words sank deep into him. *"Maybe they're right. Maybe the pastor doesn't see us anymore."*

By the time Ethan walked out of the hall, what had begun as a faint whisper had grown into a solid conviction. He wasn't angry, not yet. But the seed of doubt had been planted.

Meanwhile, Pastor David was still in the sanctuary, kneeling at the altar. He hadn't gone to the fellowship hall—he often lingered after service to pray for those who had responded to the message. He had no idea the conversations unfolding just a few feet away.

Miriam, standing by the door, overheard snippets of Clara's voice rising. Her stomach tightened. She had heard these kinds of murmurs before—small in the beginning, harmless to the untrained ear, but dangerous if left unchecked.

She quietly gathered Rachel and their son to head home, praying under her breath. *"Lord, cover us. Let not the whispers grow louder than Your voice."*

But by the evening, the whispers had already traveled across phone calls and dining room tables. What began as dissatisfaction in one corner had begun to weave its way through the congregation.

The perfect Sunday was unraveling into something else.

REFLECTION

Whispers may seem small, but they carry the power to shape perceptions and divide hearts. Hurt that is magnified without grace can create walls between shepherd and sheep. True healing comes when concerns are brought with love, not spread in secret.

> **"Let no corrupt communication proceed out of your mouth, but that which is good to the use of edifying, that it may minister grace unto the hearers." (Ephesians 4:29 - KJV).**

> **"Where no wood is, there the fire goeth out: so where there is no talebearer, the strife ceaseth." (Proverbs 26:20 - KJV).**

Chapter 3

Behind the Parsonage Door

The ride home from church was unusually quiet. The children, Rachel and her younger brother Micah, exchanged glances in the back seat, sensing the silence pressing in like a heavy fog. Pastor David kept his eyes fixed on the road, hands gripping the steering wheel tighter than usual.

Miriam sat beside him, her lips moving silently in prayer. She could read her husband as easily as the pages of her Bible. The sermon had been powerful, the altar call full, but something in his spirit was unsettled. She had caught fragments of Clara's whispers, seen the subtle shift in faces during fellowship. He hadn't. Not yet.

When they arrived at the parsonage, David dropped his keys on the table with a sigh that seemed to come from the depths of his soul. His shoulders slumped as if the weight of the congregation had climbed into the car and followed him home.

"Dinner will be ready soon," Miriam said softly, hoping to break the heaviness.

David nodded, but instead of sitting at the table, he walked straight into the small study off the living room and closed the door. Through the thin walls, Rachel heard the muffled sound of her father's voice. At first, she thought he was on the phone, but then she recognized the tone—it was prayer, weary and strained.

"Lord, I gave them everything today. Why does it still feel like it's not enough?"

Rachel froze in the hallway. Her father's voice cracked in a way she had never heard from the pulpit. She tiptoed back to her room, heart pounding. To everyone else, he was strong, unwavering, untouchable. But behind the parsonage door, he was human.

At the kitchen sink, Miriam stared out the window, her hands resting on the edge of the counter. She had prayed this prayer countless times before: "Father, guard his heart. Don't let the whispers destroy him. Give me the strength to carry what he cannot speak aloud."

Micah tugged at her sleeve. "Mom, why is Dad sad? Didn't church go good today?"

Miriam forced a smile, brushing his hair. "Yes, baby. Church went good. Sometimes, even when things look perfect, people carry heavy things inside. That's why we pray for Daddy."

Later that night, David joined them at the dinner table, his smile carefully in place, but his eyes betrayed the battle within. He asked Rachel to say grace. Her voice trembled slightly as she prayed, "Lord, bless this food, and please give Dad peace."

No one spoke after the "Amen." The family simply ate, each silently aware that the man who carried the church on his shoulders was slowly bleeding within the safety of his own home.

REFLECTION

Behind every pulpit stands a family that feels the weight of ministry too. Members see sermons, but they rarely see sleepless nights, strained smiles, or whispered prayers of exhaustion. The shepherd's burden does not end at the sanctuary door—it follows him home.

> **"Bear ye one another's burdens, and so fulfil the law of Christ." (Galatians 6:2 - KJV).**
>
> **"Obey them that have the rule over you, and submit yourselves: for they watch for your souls, as they that must give account, that they may do it with joy, and not with grief: for that is unprofitable for you." (Hebrews 13:17 - KJV).**

Chapter 4

A Daughter's Silent Tears

Wednesday evening came, and the church lights glowed against the dark sky. Rachel had grown used to sitting on the front pew while her father led Bible study, but tonight felt different. She carried the heaviness of Sunday with her, the sound of his cracked prayer echoing in her mind.

Before service began, Rachel lingered in the foyer, flipping through her Bible. A group of women gathered nearby, their voices hushed but sharp enough to pierce. "I just don't understand," Sister Clara whispered. "If pastor really cared, he'd be more available. My cousin's pastor visits his members weekly. Why can't ours?"

Another voice chimed in, "And his daughter—look at her. She sits up front like she's a little saint. But does she even know what the members go through?"

Rachel's face flushed hot. She pretended to keep reading, though the words blurred on the page. *"They're talking about Dad...and me."*

She slipped into the sanctuary before tears could fall. Her father stood at the pulpit, smiling as he welcomed the congregation. To everyone else, he looked confident and strong, but Rachel knew the truth. She had seen his weary eyes at the dinner table, heard his broken prayer through the study door.

As he opened in prayer, Rachel bowed her head, gripping the Bible tight against her chest. She whispered, *"God, why are they so mean? Don't they see how much he loves them?"*

The service went on, songs sung, scriptures read, and lessons taught. But Rachel's heart remained heavy. She was only a teenager, yet she was already carrying wounds that the congregation would never acknowledge. Wounds not from strangers in the world but from the very church her family gave their lives to serve.

That night at home, she cried silently into her pillow. Her tears didn't come because of her father's preaching, but because of the careless words she couldn't un-hear.

She didn't tell her parents. She didn't want to add to their burden. So Rachel carried the hurt alone—quiet, hidden, shaping her heart in ways no one saw.

REFLECTION

Children of pastors often bear silent wounds. While members magnify their own hurts, they forget that words and whispers can cut deep into the hearts of the pastor's family. The shepherd bleeds, but so do his children.

> **"But I say unto you, That every idle word that men shall speak, they shall give account thereof in the day of judgment." (Matthew 12:36 - KJV).**

"But whoso shall offend one of these little ones which believe in me, it were better for him that a millstone were hanged about his neck, and that he were drowned in the depth of the sea." (Matthew 18:6 - KJV).

Chapter 5

The Burden of Expectations

Thursday morning found Pastor David already awake before dawn. He sat at his desk, Bible open, sermon notes scattered across the surface. The clock ticked steadily, but his mind felt rushed by the unspoken demands he carried.

His phone buzzed with a new message:

- *"Pastor, can you meet me today at lunch? It's urgent."*
- *"Pastor, my son is in trouble again. Please call."*
- *"Pastor, we need you at the hospital tonight."*

Each request was genuine, but they piled one on top of another like bricks on his chest. He rubbed his temples and whispered, *"Lord, how do I do it all?"*

By mid-morning, Miriam walked into the study carrying a cup of coffee. She placed it gently on the desk and looked at him with concern.

"David, you can't keep this pace. You haven't slept properly in weeks."

He forced a small smile. "They need me, Miriam. That's the call. If I don't show up, they'll think I don't care."

Her eyes softened but carried quiet fire. "And what about us? What about Rachel and Micah? What about you?"

David's smile faded. He wanted to answer, but the truth was heavy: the congregation expected him to be a shepherd without limits, a counselor without rest, a preacher without flaws, a father to every child, all while being a husband and father at home.

Later that day, he sat with a member in the hospital, listening patiently. By evening, he was back at the church for a board meeting. He returned home long after the children had gone to bed. Rachel had left a note on his desk: *Goodnight, Dad. I miss you.*

He read it twice, tears welling. He had spent his entire day pouring into others, yet his own daughter longed for his presence.

The burden of expectations was crushing—no room for weakness, no margin for rest. The people magnified their own hurts, but minimized the cracks spreading through their pastor's life.

REFLECTION

Pastors are called to serve, but they are not called to be superhuman. Congregations often magnify their own needs while overlooking the shepherd's humanity. Ministry must be carried with balance, or the weight of expectations will crush both leader and family.

> **"Come unto me, all ye that labour and are heavy laden, and I will give you rest." (Matthew 11:28 - KJV).**

"**Remember them which have the rule over you, who have spoken unto you the word of God: whose faith follow, considering the end of their conversation.**" **(Hebrews 13:7 - KJV).**

Chapter 6

The Confrontation

The Sunday afternoon sun streamed through the stained-glass windows as the last few members left the sanctuary. Pastor David was gathering his notes when he noticed Ethan waiting near the front pew. Ethan's arms were folded, his expression tight with something unsaid.

"Pastor, do you have a minute?" Ethan asked, his voice polite but firm.

"Of course, brother," David replied, motioning toward the front row. They both sat, the sanctuary suddenly feeling heavier than it had during worship.

Ethan cleared his throat. "Some of us, well, we've been talking. People feel you're distant lately. Sister Helen said you didn't visit after her surgery. And others are upset you've canceled Bible study before. We just don't feel… cared for the way we used to."

The words hit David like stones, each one echoing louder than the last. He clasped his hands, nodding slowly. "I understand the concern. I truly do. But Ethan, I've been doing my best. I was at the hospital twice last week. I've counseled marriages late into the night. And I've tried to balance that with being present for Miriam and the children. It isn't easy."

Ethan shifted uncomfortably but pressed on. "I know you have a family, pastor, but the church needs you. That's why you're here. We can't be neglected."

David looked down at his hands. Neglected. The word sliced through him. He thought of the hours poured out in prayer, the countless phone calls, the visits nobody noticed. Neglected? He had given everything—and still it wasn't enough.

After a long silence, he said softly, "I hear your concerns. I'll do what I can."

Ethan nodded, satisfied, and left.

David sat alone in the sanctuary, staring at the empty seats. His heart was heavy, his spirit crushed. He whispered into the emptiness, *"Lord, what more can I give? They see their pain, but do they see mine?"*

From the balcony, Miriam quietly watched. She hadn't heard every word, but she could read the weight on her husband's shoulders. She clasped her hands and whispered, "Father, hold him together when others pull him apart."

The confrontation was over but the wound remained.

REFLECTION

Confrontations in the church can be holy moments for healing—or heavy blows that deepen wounds. Too often, members magnify their grievances while minimizing the sacrifices their pastors already carry. A shepherd is not called to meet every demand but to faithfully follow God's leading.

> **"But if ye bite and devour one another, take heed that ye be not consumed one of another." (Galatians 5:15 - KJV).**

> **"And let us consider one another to provoke unto love and to good works." (Hebrews 10:24 - KJV).**

Chapter 7

Miriam's Breaking Point

The parsonage was quiet, but Miriam's spirit was anything but. She stood in the kitchen long after dinner dishes had been washed and put away, staring blankly at the window above the sink. The night sky was clear, the stars glimmering faintly, but her eyes were blurred with unshed tears.

She had watched David come home carrying more than his Bible. He carried the weight of another conversation that left him hollow. Ethan's words—though spoken in a respectful tone—had drained him. Miriam didn't need to hear the details; she saw it in his eyes, in the heaviness of his steps, in the way he avoided the children's questions at the table.

She dried her hands on a towel and leaned against the counter. *"How long, Lord?"* she whispered into the stillness. *"How long must we live like this?"*

Being a pastor's wife was a role she had accepted with grace years ago, but lately it felt more like an invisible battlefield. People expected her to smile at every service, to host with perfection, to stand at her husband's side as though the whispers never reached her ears. But they did. And every word carried a sting.

Miriam remembered the early days of ministry—when she and David prayed in their tiny living room about answering God's call. She had said yes, believing she was strong enough. But she hadn't known that strength would mean enduring sleepless nights alone while her husband counseled members until dawn. She hadn't realized her children would grow up under the magnifying glass of a congregation that judged their every move.

She thought of Rachel, who had come to her last night with quiet tears. "Mom, why do people talk bad about Dad if he's helping them?" Miriam had hugged her tightly, unable to answer in a way that would make sense to a teenage heart.

Then there was Micah, still small enough to cling to his father's leg when he left for another hospital visit, asking, "Dad, do you have to go again? Can't you stay with us?"

David always kissed his forehead and said, "I'll be back soon," but soon often turned into hours, even days of absence.

Miriam felt the breaking point creeping closer every day. She was tired of smiling through judgmental stares, tired of hearing that her husband was "not enough," tired of being strong for everyone else while no one asked how she was doing.

She sank into a chair at the table, burying her face in her hands. Hot tears spilled freely now. "Lord, I'm weary. I know You called David, but did You call us to be invisible casualties?"

Upstairs, David was praying in the study. His voice drifted down faintly: "God, give me strength. Don't let me fail them."

Miriam lifted her head. For a moment, she wanted to scream at the ceiling: *"What about us? Don't let us fail too!"* But the words stayed locked in her chest.

Instead, she opened her worn Bible and let it fall to the Psalms. Her eyes landed on a verse she had read many times: **"I am forgotten as a dead man out of mind: I am like a broken vessel." (Psalm 31:12 - KJV).** It was as if David's heart cry had become her own.

That night, when she finally slipped into bed beside her husband, Miriam stared into the darkness. He was already asleep, his breathing heavy, exhaustion pulling him into rest. She whispered into the silence, *"Lord, heal us before this ministry breaks us."*

For the first time in years, Miriam wondered if she could keep going. The calling was sacred, yes—but at what cost?

REFLECTION

Behind every pastor stands a spouse who carries silent wounds. The congregation sees the sermons and smiles, but rarely the tears shed in secret. Pastors' wives and husbands are often the unseen warriors—bearing burdens, absorbing criticism, and fighting battles no one acknowledges. Their breaking points are real, and their healing matters too.

> **"Be kindly affectioned one to another with brotherly love; in honour preferring one another." (Romans 12:10 - KJV).**

"Two are better than one; because they have a good reward for their labour. For if they fall, the one will lift up his fellow..." (Ecclesiastes 4:9–10 - KJV).

Chapter 8

When Shepherds Bleed

The house was quiet long after midnight. Miriam and the children had drifted into uneasy sleep, but Pastor David remained in his study. The lamp on his desk cast a dim glow over a stack of unopened mail, a Bible with its pages worn thin, and a leather-bound journal that held secrets no one else knew.

He opened the journal slowly, as if each page carried weight. With his pen in hand, he began to write—his script uneven, words heavy with exhaustion.

"Lord, tonight I feel like an empty vessel. I pour and pour, but I wonder if there's anything left inside me. They say I don't care, but if they only knew the nights I've driven across town in silence, praying the whole way. If they only knew the times I've left my children crying at the door just so I could comfort someone else's. If they only knew the tears Miriam has wiped from my eyes when the house was quiet. Do they know? Do they care?"

David set down the pen, rubbing his eyes. The accusations, though subtle, echoed louder in the stillness of night. Neglectful. Distant. Uncaring. Each word felt like a dagger to the heart of a man who had sacrificed nearly everything for the people he served.

He turned the pages of his Bible, desperate for comfort. His eyes landed on the story of Paul in 2 Corinthians: **"In labours more abundant, in stripes above measure, in prisons more frequent, in deaths oft…"** David whispered aloud, *"Paul, you bled for them too."*

He leaned back in his chair, closing his eyes. Memories flooded his mind—the first sermon he ever preached, the day the congregation laid hands on him and called him "God's chosen shepherd." The weight of that moment had felt holy. But now, years later, that same weight felt crushing.

David picked up his pen again.

"Ministry feels like bleeding without bandages. I smile for them, I preach for them, I stand strong for them, but inside… I am bleeding. And when a shepherd bleeds, who tends his wounds? Who notices? They magnify their pain but minimize mine. Lord, am I allowed to be broken? Or must I always wear the armor, even when it's crushing me?"

The clock ticked past two in the morning. His head drooped into his hands. He wanted to scream, to release the ache that had built up over years of silent sacrifice. But instead, he wept. Deep, shuddering sobs that no one heard—not Miriam, not the children, not the congregation who would expect him to stand tall again by Sunday.

In the privacy of his study, David was not Pastor, Reverend, or Shepherd. He was simply a man—a man who loved God, loved people, and yet felt broken under the weight of both.

When the tears finally slowed, he wrote one last line before closing the journal: *"Shepherds bleed too. Lord, please don't let me bleed to death in silence."*

He blew out the lamp and sat in the darkness, his heart aching, his spirit weary. Tomorrow he would preach again. Tomorrow he would smile. Tomorrow he would carry the church on his shoulders once more. But tonight, only God saw the bleeding of His shepherd.

REFLECTION

Pastors often suffer silently. They preach life while battling their own despair. They comfort others while no one notices their own pain. They bleed behind closed doors, unseen and unacknowledged. Yet even when no one else sees, God does. And He is the Shepherd who binds up the wounds of His under-shepherds.

> **"He healeth the broken in heart, and bindeth up their wounds." (Psalm 147:3 - KJV).**

> **"For we have not an high priest which cannot be touched with the feeling of our infirmities..." (Hebrews 4:15 - KJV).**

Chapter 9

God's Perspective

He sat in the darkness of his study, head bowed, tears still damp on his cheeks. The house slept, the city was silent, and only his weary prayers lingered in the air.

But heaven was not silent.

If David could have heard beyond his exhaustion, he might have sensed it—the steady heartbeat of the Father, the voice of the One who called him long before a congregation ever voted him in, the Shepherd of shepherds who saw every wound, every sacrifice, every tear.

"Son, I see you."

The words were not spoken aloud, yet they pressed gently into his heart.

"I saw you when you left your child's birthday to pray for another family's crisis. I saw you when you drove through the night to sit at a hospital bedside while your own body begged for rest. I saw you when you smiled through sermons, though your spirit was weary. You are not invisible to Me."

Scriptures he had preached countless times now spoke back to him. **"For God is not unrighteous to forget your work and labour of love…" (Hebrews 6:10 - KJV).**

David whispered into the stillness, *"But Lord, they don't understand. They think I don't care."*

The gentle voice of God replied: *"Did they understand My Son? He healed their sick, fed their hungry, raised their dead, yet they said He had a devil. He came to His own, and His own received Him not. You are not rejected because you are unfaithful—you are rejected because you are walking in My steps."*

Tears welled again, but this time not only from sorrow. A strange comfort wrapped around him, as though the words were bandages binding wounds he thought would never close.

"Shepherd, even when your flock misunderstands you, remember: I am the Good Shepherd. I know My sheep, and I am known of Mine. And I know you. I know your heart."

David lifted his head, his mind drifting to Moses—misunderstood by Israel though he led them out of bondage. To Jeremiah—mocked for speaking truth though his heart broke for his people. To Paul—stoned, beaten, shipwrecked, yet still pressing on. And above them all, to Jesus—who poured out love only to be despised and rejected.

"Lord," David whispered, *"I am not greater than they."*

A warmth filled the room, though the air was still.

"No, son, you are not greater than they. But you are not lesser either. I called you. And I will carry you. They may magnify their wounds and minimize yours, but I see every cut, every bruise, every hidden tear. You are mine. And I will bind up your brokenness."

The silence of the study became holy. For the first time in weeks, David felt peace stir inside him. He was still bleeding, yes. The whispers had not stopped, the burdens had not lifted. But now he remembered—he was not carrying them alone.

Miriam, asleep upstairs, shifted in her rest. Rachel's face, tear-stained from her own silent prayers, pressed into her pillow. Even they were not unseen. The same God who saw the shepherd's wounds also saw the family's.

He wrote one more line in his journal before closing it for the night: *"Heaven sees. That is enough."*

REFLECTION

When leaders are misunderstood, when pastors are rejected, when families are wounded in silence, heaven is not blind. God sees what people overlook. He knows what others minimize. And His voice whispers to every weary shepherd: *"I see you. I called you. And I will carry you."*

> **"For the eyes of the Lord run to and fro throughout the whole earth, to shew himself strong in the behalf of them whose heart is perfect toward him." (2 Chronicles 16:9 - KJV).**

"Behold, I have graven thee upon the palms of my hands; thy walls are continually before me." (Isaiah 49:16 - KJV).

"The LORD is my shepherd; I shall not want. He restoreth my soul…" (Psalm 23:1, 3 - KJV).

Chapter 10

The Path to Healing

The following Sunday dawned bright and warm, but the air in Grace Tabernacle Church carried a strange heaviness. The sanctuary filled as usual, yet conversations were clipped, laughter muted. The whispers that had begun in corners now hung in the atmosphere like a shadow.

Pastor David stood behind the pulpit, his Bible open, but his eyes lifted heavenward. He had wrestled all week—through sleepless nights, journal pages filled with tears, and whispered reassurances from God's Spirit. Now, as he faced his flock, he felt a quiet resolve.

He began softly, his voice carrying a different weight than before.

"Church, I want to share something from my heart today. I know some of you feel neglected, overlooked, or unseen. And I hear you. But I need you to know—your shepherd bleeds too."

The sanctuary went silent. Every head lifted, every whisper stilled.

"I have prayed for you when you didn't know. I have sat with you in your darkest hours. I have carried your names before God when you were unaware. But sometimes, while carrying you, I have broken inside. Sometimes, while helping you heal, my own family has been hurting." His voice cracked slightly, but he did not stop.

Miriam sat in the front pew, her hands clasped tight, tears streaming silently. Rachel leaned against her, her young heart pounding. For the first time, the congregation was hearing the truth she had known all along.

Ethan, seated a few rows back, felt his chest tighten. The words he had spoken to pastor replayed in his mind—not as a bold defense of the congregation, but as daggers he had unknowingly thrust into a weary heart. Shame washed over him.

Pastor David continued, "I don't say this to make you feel guilty. I say this because we need each other. A church cannot thrive when the shepherd carries the weight alone. We must walk together—bearing one another's burdens, loving one another, forgiving one another."

From the back, Clara shifted uncomfortably. Her arms crossed tightly, her eyes darted around the room, but the conviction of the Spirit was undeniable. She whispered under her breath, *"I only wanted to be heard..."* But even she could feel the Spirit's gentle rebuke.

David closed his Bible and stepped down from the pulpit. "If we are truly family, then healing must begin here. Not just for the members. Not just for the pastor. But for all of us."

The altar filled slowly at first—then suddenly. Ethan was the first to kneel, his shoulders shaking as he cried, "Forgive me, pastor. Forgive me, Lord. I didn't see what you were carrying." Others followed, one after another, until the front of the church was lined with both sheep and shepherd, broken together before the Shepherd of all.

Rachel knelt beside her father, slipping her hand into his. He looked down and met her eyes—eyes filled with tears but also hope. For the first time, she felt seen, her pain acknowledged not only by her family but by the church that had once wounded her.

Miriam stood, lifting her hands in worship. The heaviness she had carried for years seemed to lift as the sanctuary filled with weeping, prayers, and whispered reconciliations. She whispered to herself, "Thank You, Lord. You're healing what I thought was shattered beyond repair."

The service ended not with a sermon but with reconciliation. Hugs were exchanged, apologies spoken, prayers whispered over one another. For once, the hurt of both pastor and people was acknowledged equally.

It was not a perfect resolution—there would still be challenges, still be misunderstandings, still be moments of pain. But healing had begun.

And that was enough.

REFLECTION

True healing in the church comes when shepherd and sheep recognize that hurt is not one-sided. Members hurt. Pastors hurt. Families hurt. Healing begins when everyone acknowledges the pain and chooses grace over gossip, prayer over criticism, unity over division.

> **"Bear ye one another's burdens, and so fulfil the law of Christ." (Galatians 6:2 - KJV).**

> **"And be ye kind one to another, tenderhearted, forgiving one another, even as God for Christ's sake hath forgiven you." (Ephesians 4:32 - KJV).**

> **"Endeavouring to keep the unity of the Spirit in the bond of peace." (Ephesians 4:3 - KJV).**

Conclusion

When Hurt Finds Healing

Church hurt is one of the deepest wounds a believer can carry, as it comes from the very place where we expect to find love, safety, and grace. When offenses rise in the workplace or the marketplace, we may brush them aside. But when they come from within the house of God, they pierce the heart in a unique way. Words whispered in church hallways echo louder than shouts in the world.

This story has walked us through the unseen realities of both sides of hurt. We have watched members magnify their pain, longing to be noticed, understood, and cared for. We have also witnessed the overlooked wounds of the pastor and his family—silent tears shed behind closed doors, children scarred by gossip, a spouse stretched to the breaking point, and a shepherd who bleeds quietly while carrying the burdens of others.

It is tempting to ask, *"Whose pain matters more? The members or the pastor's?"* But the truth is that all hurt matters. Pain is not a competition. Suffering is not a contest. When one part of the body aches, the whole body suffers (see 1 Corinthians 12:26). And the church is not whole when the pain of one group is magnified while the pain of another is minimized.

The truth is, pastors are not superhuman. They are men and women with families, emotions, limitations, and scars. Their calling is divine, but their hearts are human. They stand behind pulpits with a smile, but sometimes that smile hides a thousand silent battles. When members forget this reality, expectations become crushing, criticisms cut deeper, and gossip becomes poison.

At the same time, members must not be dismissed. Their hurt is not invalid simply because the pastor carries burdens. Sheep need care. Congregants need love. Followers need shepherds. And when their wounds are minimized, bitterness grows, divisions form, and the church loses the bond of unity that Christ prayed for.

Healing begins when both sides see each other clearly, when members recognize that pastors and their families are not immune to pain; when pastors acknowledge that sheep can feel neglected or unseen. Healing begins when the church stops whispering and starts talking—in love, in honesty, in humility.

Forgiveness must flow both ways. Grace must be extended generously. Unity must be pursued intentionally. The world outside is watching. They do not need to see perfect churches; they need to see forgiving churches. They need to witness communities where wounds are acknowledged, burdens are shared, and love covers a multitude of sins (see 1 Peter 4:8).

For pastors reading this: your hurt is real. God sees your silent tears, your sleepless nights, your sacrifices unnoticed by men. You are not alone, and you are not forgotten. Heaven has recorded every act of faithfulness, every prayer whispered on behalf of your people, every moment you chose to love instead of walk away. The Shepherd of shepherds is binding your wounds even now.

Church Hurt

For members reading this: your hurt is valid. Your needs matter. God has placed you in a spiritual family because you were never meant to walk alone. But remember this—your shepherd is not your Savior. He is a servant, chosen but human, and he cannot carry what only Christ can bear. Extend grace. Offer prayer. Guard your words. Seek unity, not division.

For pastors' families—spouses and children who live in the shadow of ministry—you are not invisible to God. The same eyes that saw Hagar weeping in the wilderness see you. He knows the weight you carry, the tears you cry, and the sacrifices you make. Your unseen faithfulness is precious to Him.

Church hurt is real. But so is church healing. And healing begins when we stop minimizing one another's pain, when we stop magnifying our own wounds above others, and when we choose the path of love, forgiveness, and reconciliation.

May every church become a place where shepherd and sheep walk together—not in competition, but in compassion. May every pastor find strength in knowing their labor is not in vain. May every member find peace in knowing their voice is heard. And may the world look upon the church, not as a place of broken promises, but as a living testimony of grace, forgiveness, and healing.

Because in the end, the church is not ours. It is His. And the Shepherd who laid down His life for the sheep is still binding wounds, still restoring souls, and still leading us all into green pastures.

FINAL SCRIPTURES FOR REFLECTION

"And above all these things put on charity, which is the bond of perfectness." (Colossians 3:14 - KJV).

"And let us not be weary in well doing: for in due season we shall reap, if we faint not." (Galatians 6:9 - KJV).

"By this shall all men know that ye are my disciples, if ye have love one to another." (John 13:35 - KJV).

www.ingramcontent.com/pod-product-compliance
Lightning Source LLC
Chambersburg PA
CBHW071759040426
42446CB00012B/2625